SCHOOLS

by Emma Bassier

Cody Koala

An Imprint of Pop!
popbooksonline.com

abdobooks.com
Published by Pop!, a division of ABDO, PO Box 398166, Minneapolis, Minnesota 55439.

Printed in the United States of America, North Mankato, Minnesota

052019
092019

THIS BOOK CONTAINS RECYCLED MATERIALS

Cover Photo: iStockphoto
Interior Photos; iStockphoto, 1, 5, 7 (top), 7 (bottom left), 7 (bottom right), 9, 10, 11, 13, 15, 16, 17, 19, 20, 21

Editor: Meg Gaertner
Series Designer: Jake Slavik

Library of Congress Control Number: 2018964653

Publisher's Cataloging-in-Publication Data
Names: Bassier, Emma, author.
Title: Schools / by Emma Bassier.
Description: Minneapolis, Minnesota : Pop!, 2020 | Series: Places in my community | Includes online resources and index.
Identifiers: ISBN 9781532163524 (lib. bdg.) | ISBN 9781532164965 (ebook)
Subjects: LCSH: Schools--Juvenile literature. | School buildings--Juvenile literature. | Community schools--Juvenile literature.
Classification: DDC 371--dc23

Hello! My name is

Cody Koala

Pop open this book and you'll find QR codes like this one, loaded with information, so you can learn even more!

Scan this code* and others like it while you read, or visit the website below to make this book pop.

popbooksonline.com/schools

*Scanning QR codes requires a web-enabled smart device with a QR code reader app and a camera.

Table of Contents

Chapter 1

Yellow Bus

A bus stops at the street corner. Several children get on. The bus brings them to school. *Brrring!* The school bell rings. The children run inside. It is time to learn.

Watch a video here!

Chapter 2

A Place to Learn

A school is where **students** go to learn. Students learn different subjects at school. Subjects are areas of learning.

Learn more here!

Preschool and kindergarten are for the youngest children. Older students are divided into **grades**. Each grade learns together. Most students in the same grade are the same age.

kindergarten

Students go to elementary school through grades 5 or 6. Then they go to middle school through grade 8.

High school is for students in grades 9 through 12.

Some schools have fewer than one hundred students. Other schools have more than one thousand!

Chapter 3

Inside a School

Students learn in **classrooms**. They sit at desks or tables. The **teacher** may write on a **whiteboard**. Or the teacher may teach with books or computers.

Complete an activity here!

Younger students may stay in the same classroom all day. Older students may move between classrooms. They learn a different subject in each one.

Students must stay in school until age 16 in most states.

whiteboard
teacher's desk
desk
chair

Many schools have a cafeteria. Students eat lunch in this room.

Some schools have a library. Students can find lots of books there.

Many schools also have a gym. Students play sports and games in this room. They do this to stay healthy.

Chapter 4

Helping People Learn

Schools are important to the community. **Students** learn about the world and its people and places. They learn about being good community members.

Learn more here!

Schools prepare students for jobs. Older students pick their favorite subject.

They learn more details about that subject. Then they get a job in that subject.

Making Connections

Text-to-Self

Have you ever been to school? What is it like? What subjects do you learn?

Text-to-Text

Have you read other books about schools? What did you learn?

Text-to-World

Schools are important to the community. What do you think would happen if there were no schools?

Glossary

classroom – a room where students learn.

grade – a group of students who learn together and are near the same age.

student – a person who goes to school to learn.

teacher – a person who guides the learning of students.

whiteboard – a hard, smooth board that people can write on with markers, and the writing can be erased.

Index

Online Resources

popbooksonline.com

Thanks for reading this Cody Koala book!

Scan this code* and others like it in this book, or visit the website below to make this book pop!

popbooksonline.com/schools

*Scanning QR codes requires a web-enabled smart device with a QR code reader app and a camera.